Hello, my name is Marlee.

About me

My name is _____.

Track your progress

Find and trace each letter to match your completed pages.

as in "wax"

Teacher note

As each letter page is completed, students trace the letter on this tracker.

OXFORD UNIVERSITY PRES

I'm hiding ... circle me when you find me on the pages.

Before you begin writing ...

Posture

- Relax your arms
- Sit back in your chair
- Make sure your back is straight.

Put your feet flat on the floor.

Pencil grip

How you hold your pencil is important.
- Hold your pencil firmly between your thumb and index finger.
- Balance the pencil on your middle finger.
- Don't grip the pencil too tightly!

Left-handed

Right-handed

Paper position

- Tilt your page.
- Use your non-writing hand to steady the paper.

Left-handed

Right-handed

OXFORD UNIVERSITY PRES

Numbers

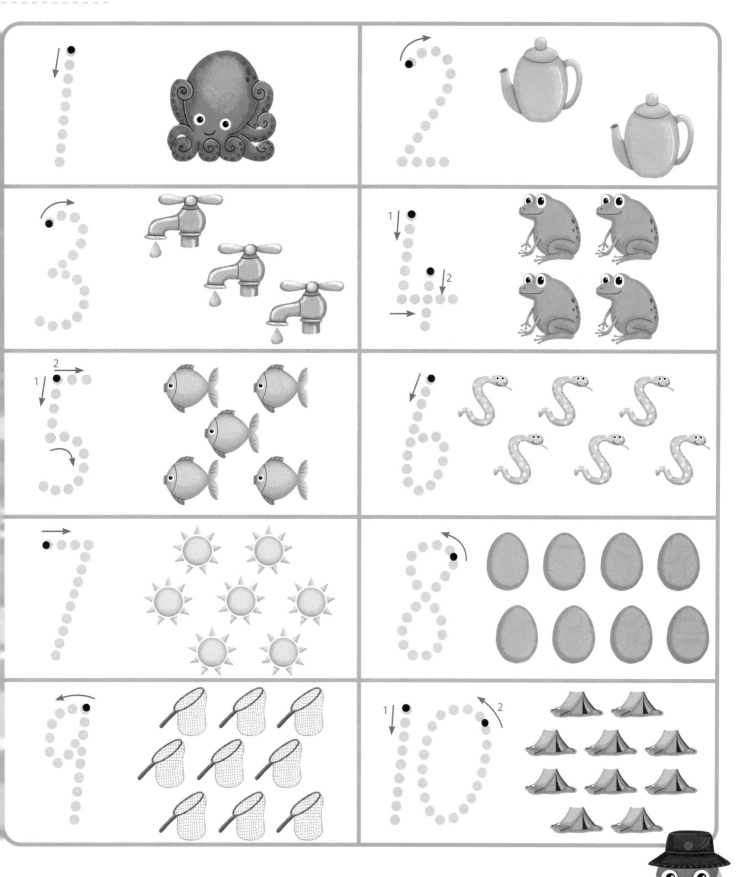

Correct number formation is essential in mathematics and should be as fluent and automatic as handwriting letters and words.

Warm-up patterns

OXFORD UNIVERSITY PRES

Track

Trace

Copy

OXFORD UNIVERSITY PRESS

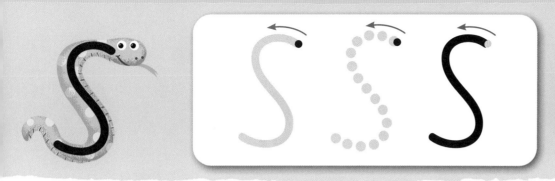

above

on

below

above

on

below

above

on

below

Fast finishers Draw a picture of something beginning with the /s/ phoneme (sound), e.g. the Sun.

Track

Trace

Copy

 • • • • •

Self-assessment!   Ask students to circle their best lower-case a and upper-case A.
Ask them to explain the reason for their choices to you or a classmate.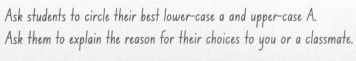

OXFORD UNIVERSITY PRESS

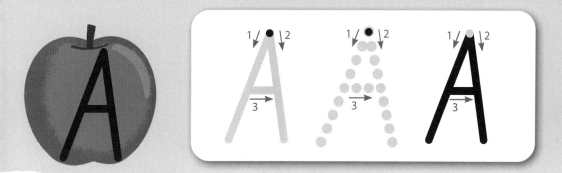

above ♪ ♩ ♫

on

below

above ♪ ♩ ♫

on

below

above ♪ ♩ ♫

on

below

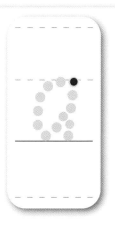

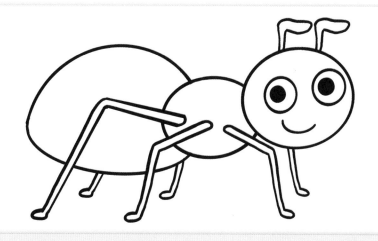

Track

Trace

Copy

OXFORD UNIVERSITY PRESS

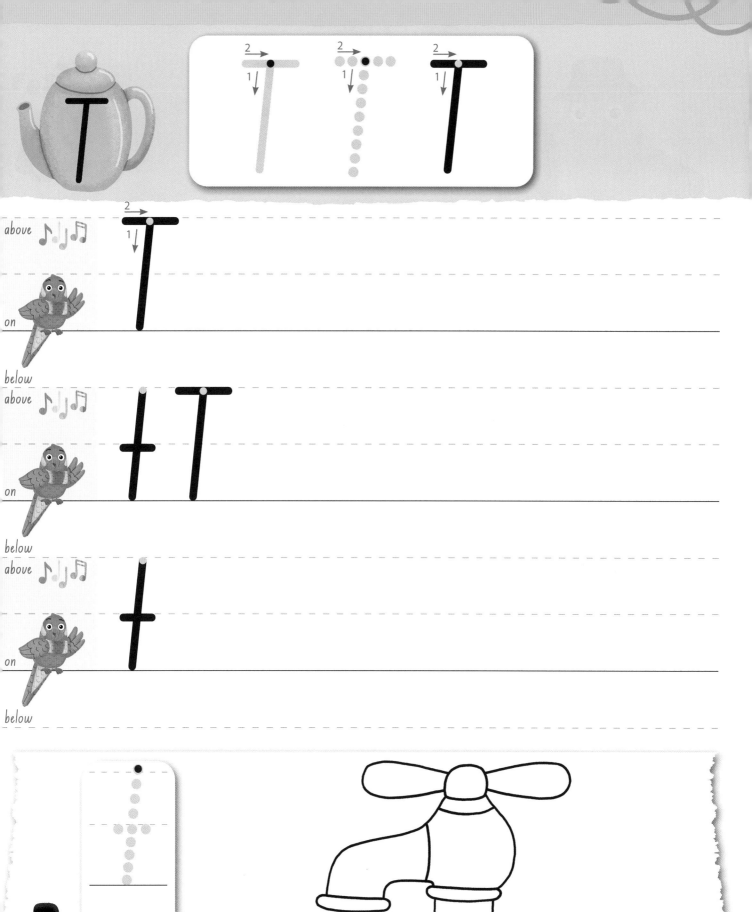

above

on

below

above

on

below

above

on

below

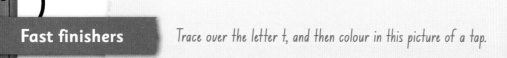

Fast finishers

Trace over the letter t, and then colour in this picture of a tap.

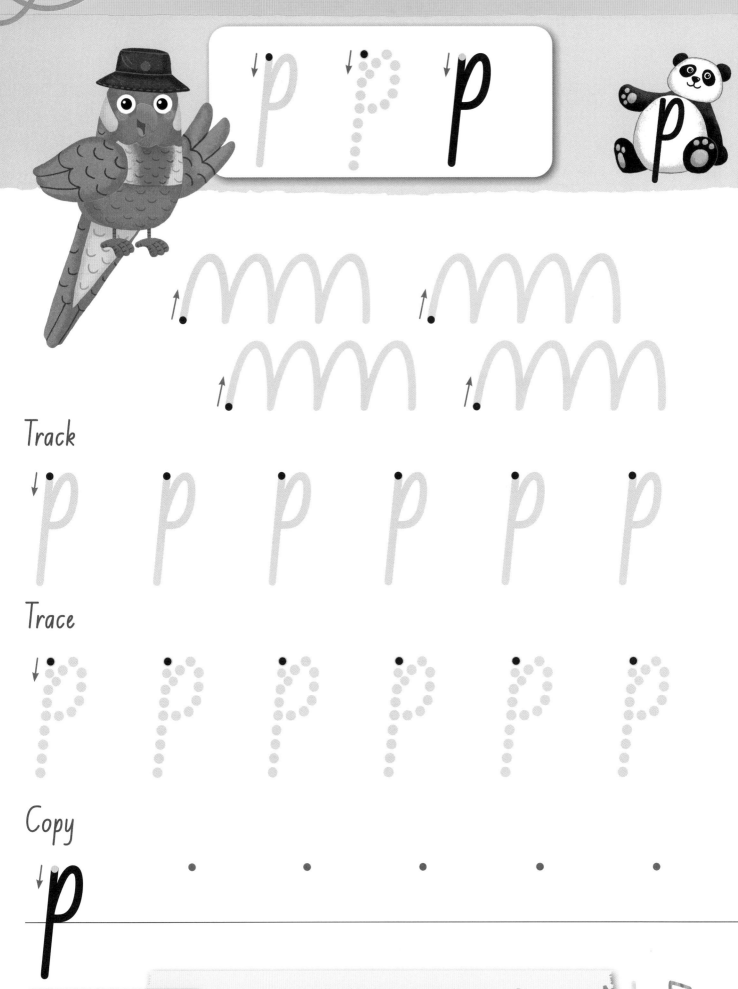

Track

Trace

Copy

Self-assessment!

Ask students to circle their best lower-case p and upper-case P.
Ask them to explain the reason for their choices to you or a classmate.

above  P

on

below

above P

on pP

below

above

on p

below

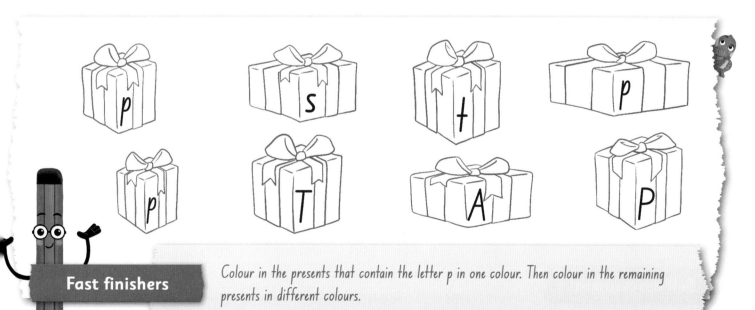

Fast finishers

Colour in the presents that contain the letter p in one colour. Then colour in the remaining presents in different colours.

pP

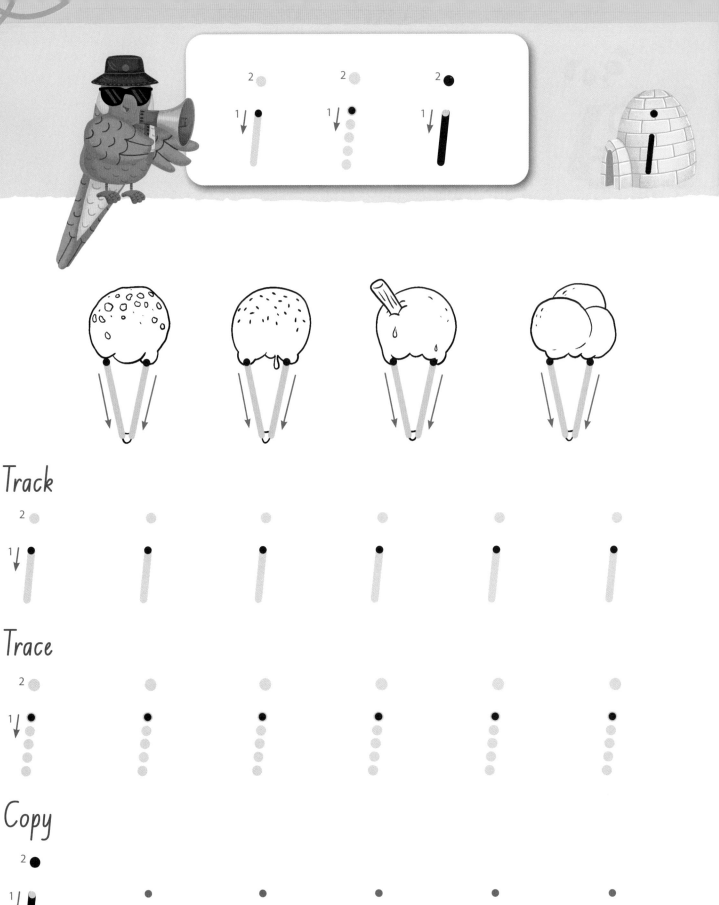

Track

Trace

Copy

Ask students to circle their best lower-case i and upper-case I.
Ask them to explain the reason for their choices to you or a classmate.

OXFORD UNIVERSITY PRESS

Colour in the insects that contain a lower-case i in one colour. Then colour in the remaining insects in different colours.

iI

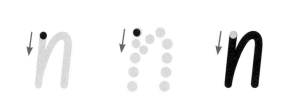

Track

Trace

Copy

OXFORD UNIVERSITY PRESS

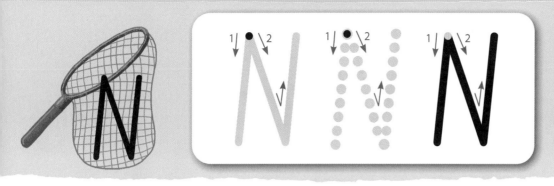

above

on

below

above

on

below

above

on

below

Fast finishers   Trace over the word "nap", and then colour in the picture of the child having a nap.

nN 19

m m **m**

Track

m m m m m m m

Trace

m m m m m m

Copy

m · · · · ·

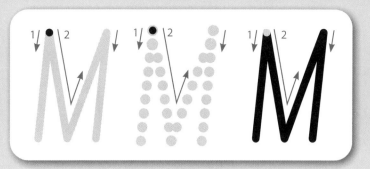

above ♪♩♫

on

below

above ♪♩♫

on

below

above ♪♩♫

M

mM

m

on

below

Fast finishers Colour in the monkeys that contain a lower-case m in one colour. Then colour in the remaining monkeys in different colours.

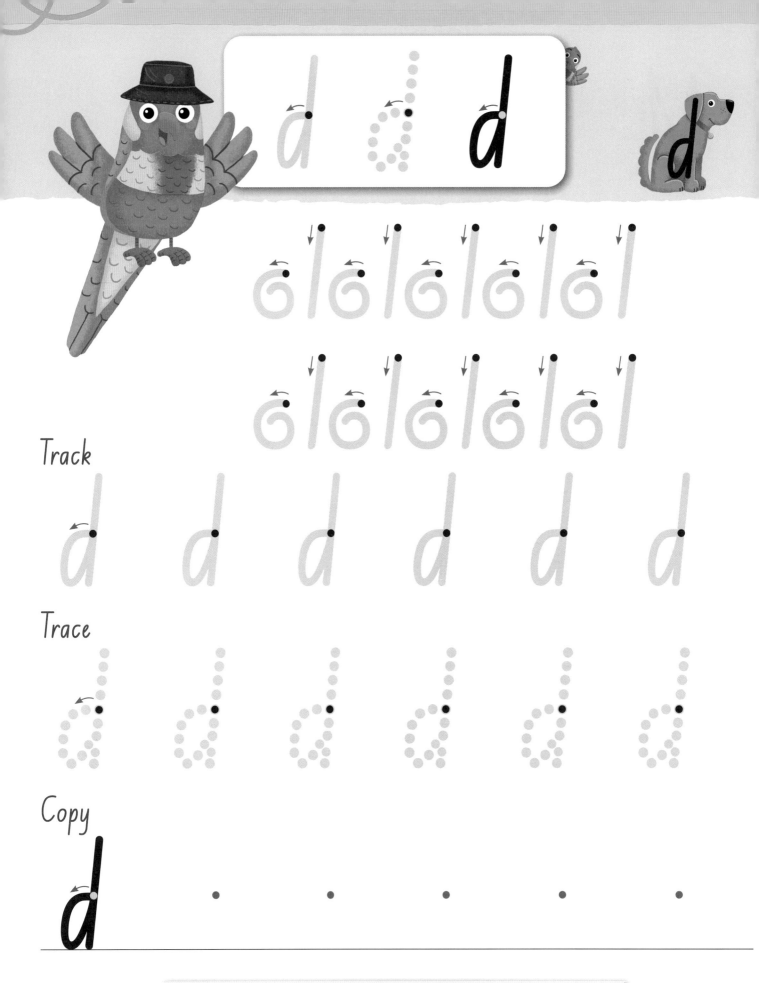

Track

Trace

Copy

OXFORD UNIVERSITY PRESS

D

dD

d

above

on

below

Fast finishers   Trace over the names, and then colour in the drawing of Sam and her dad.

OXFORD UNIVERSITY PRESS

dD   23

g

Track

g g g g g g

Trace

g g g g g g

Copy

g · · · · ·

Self-assessment!

Ask students to circle their best lower-case g and upper-case G.
Ask them to explain the reason for their choices to you or a classmate.

24

OXFORD UNIVERSITY PRESS

above

on

below

above

on

below

above

on

below

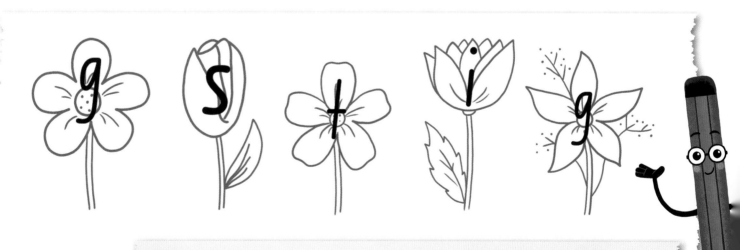

Colour in the flowers that contain a lower-case g in one colour. Then colour in the remaining flowers in different colours.

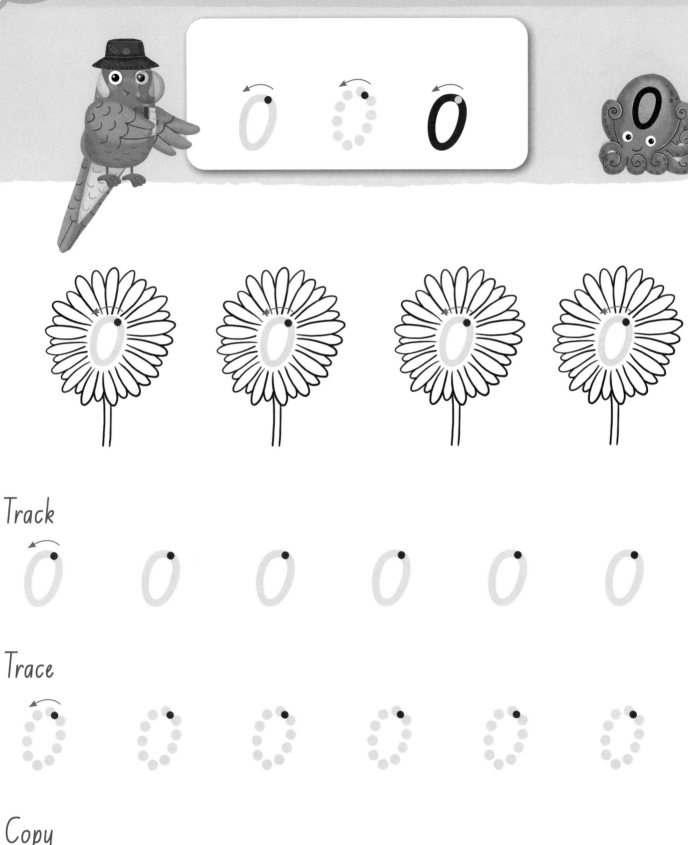

Track

Trace

Copy

OXFORD UNIVERSITY PRESS

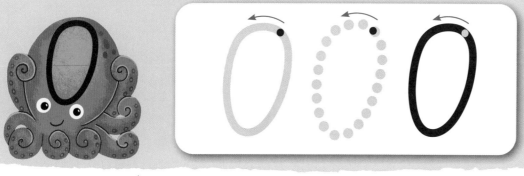

above 🎵🎵🎵 O

on

below

above 🎵🎵🎵 oO

on

below

above 🎵🎵🎵 o

on

below

Fast finishers   Find the oranges with a lower-case o inside them, and then colour them in.

Track

Trace

Copy

 • • • • •

OXFORD UNIVERSITY PRESS

above

on

below

above

on

below

above

on

below

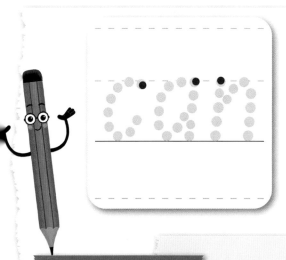

Fast finishers   Trace the word "can", and then draw something you can do.

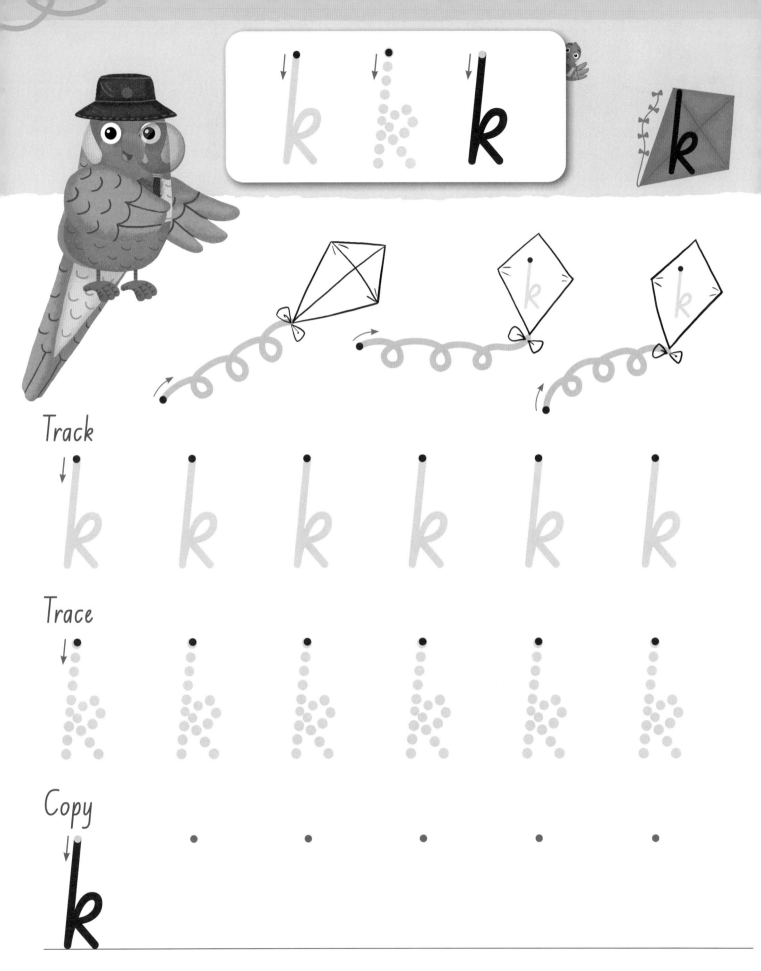

k k k

Track

k k k k k k

Trace

k k k k k k

Copy

k

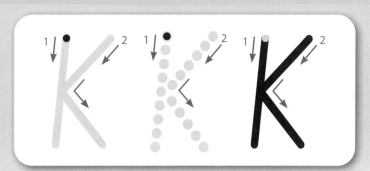

above ♪♪♫ K

on

below

above ♪♪♫ kK

on

below

above ♪♪♫ k

on

below

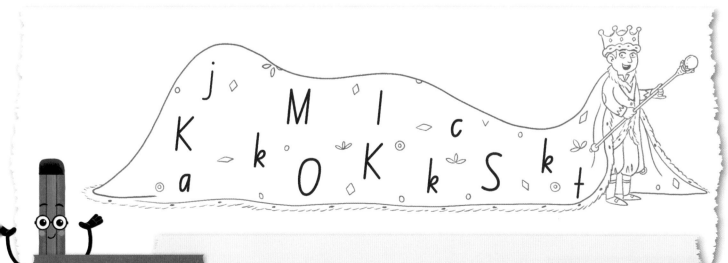

Fast finishers   Circle the lower-case k's on the king's train, and then colour in the picture.

Track

Trace

Copy

 • • • • •

Self-assessment!   Ask students to circle their best lower-case e and upper-case E.
Ask them to explain the reason for their choices to you or a classmate.

OXFORD UNIVERSITY PRESS

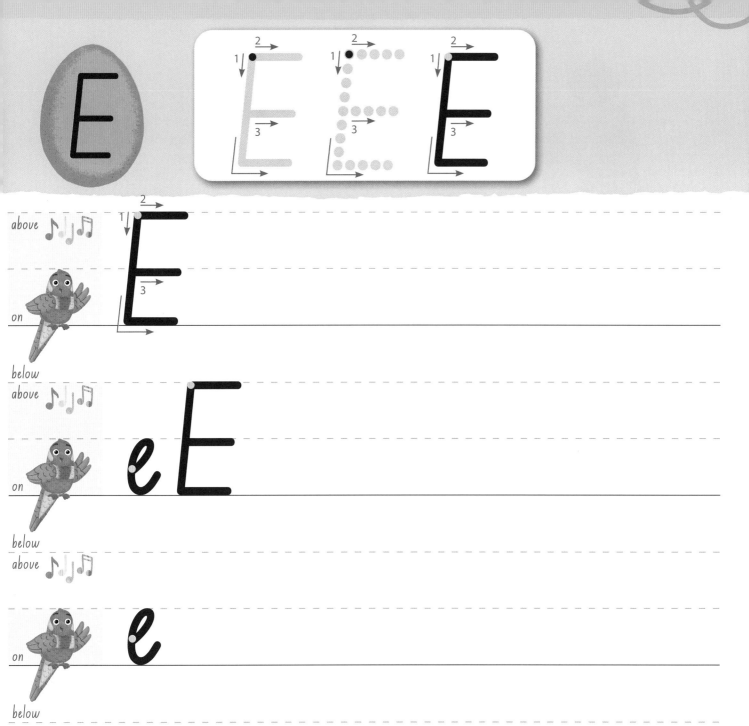

above

on

below

above

on

below

above

on

below

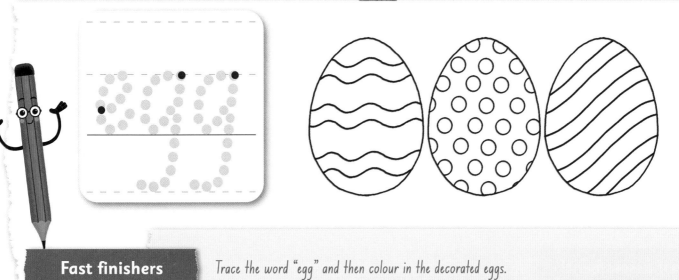

Trace the word "egg" and then colour in the decorated eggs.

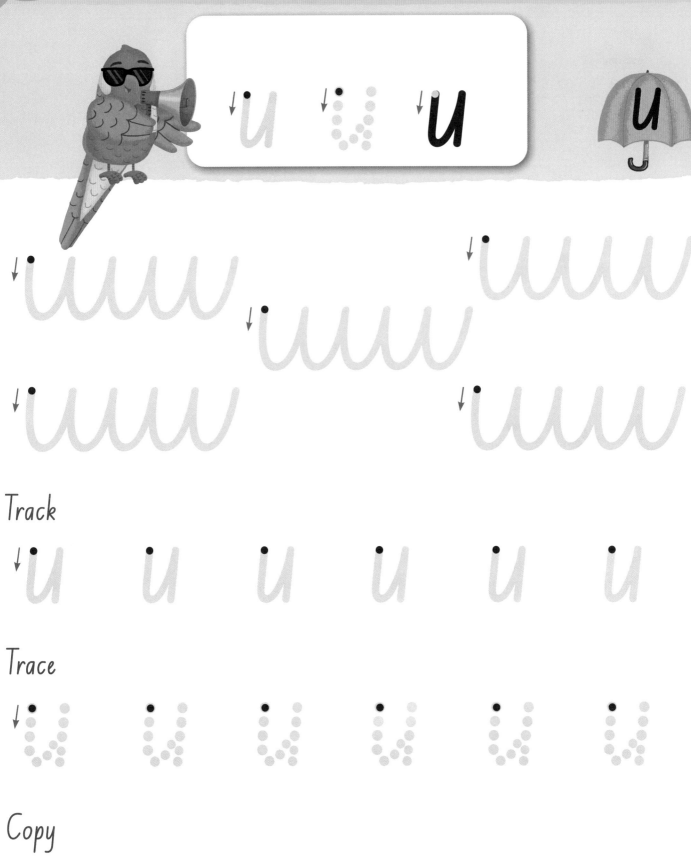

Track

Trace

Copy

Self-assessment!

Ask students to circle their best lower-case u and upper-case U.
Ask them to explain the reason for their choices to you or a classmate.

OXFORD UNIVERSITY PRESS

above ♪♩♩♫

on

below

above ♪♩♩♫

on

below

above ♪♩♩♫

on

below

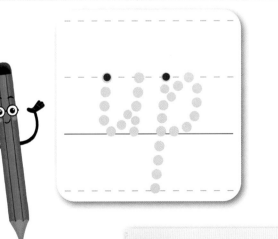

Fast finishers

Trace the word "up", and then colour in the arrow. Draw something that goes up. For example, a balloon, a lift or a crane.

r r **r**

Track

r r r r r r

Trace

r r r r r r

Copy

r

Self-assessment!

Ask students to circle their best lower-case r and upper-case R.
Ask them to explain the reason for their choices to you or a classmate.

OXFORD UNIVERSITY PRESS

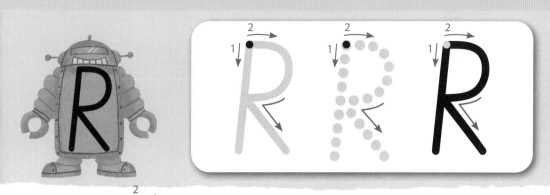

above R

on R

below

above rR

on rR

below

above

on r

below

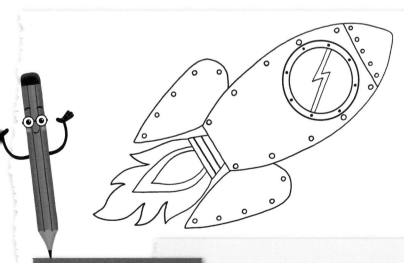

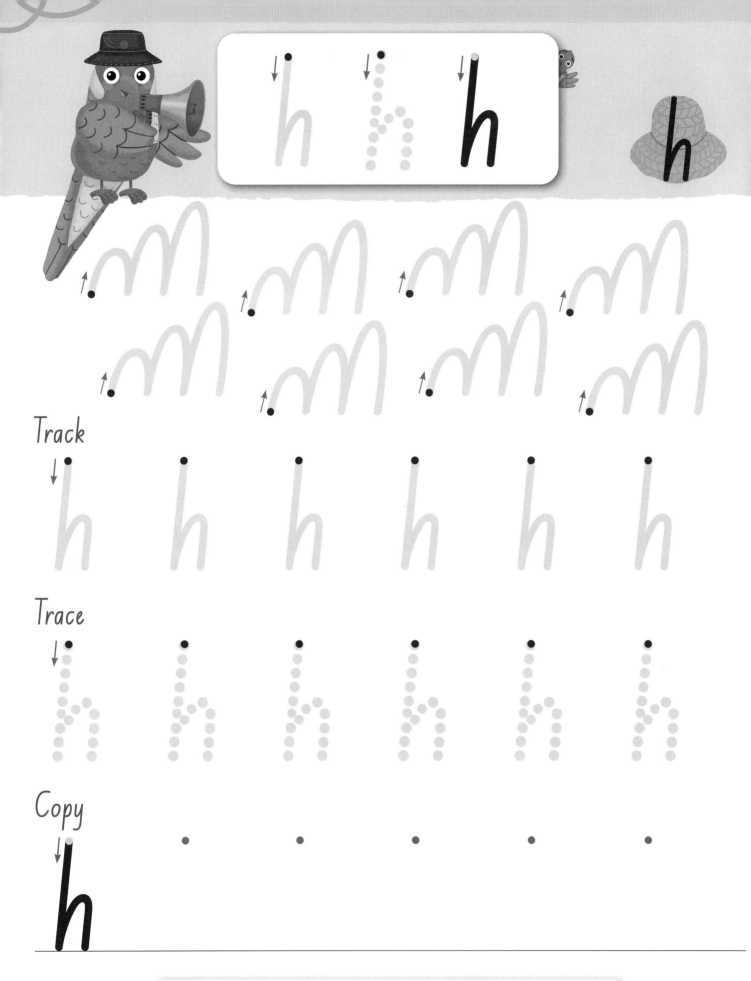

Track

Trace

Copy

Ask students to circle their best lower-case h and upper-case H.
Ask them to explain the reason for their choices to you or a classmate.

OXFORD UNIVERSITY PRESS

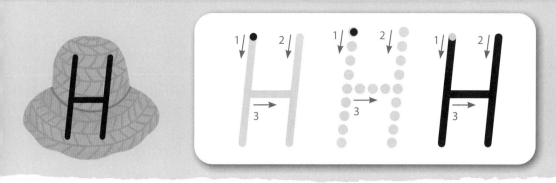

above ♪♩♩♫

H

on

below

above ♪♩♩♫

hH

on

below

above ♪♩♩♫

h

on

below

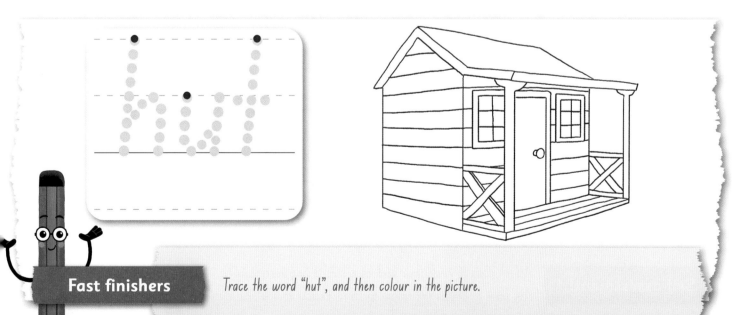

Fast finishers   Trace the word "hut", and then colour in the picture.

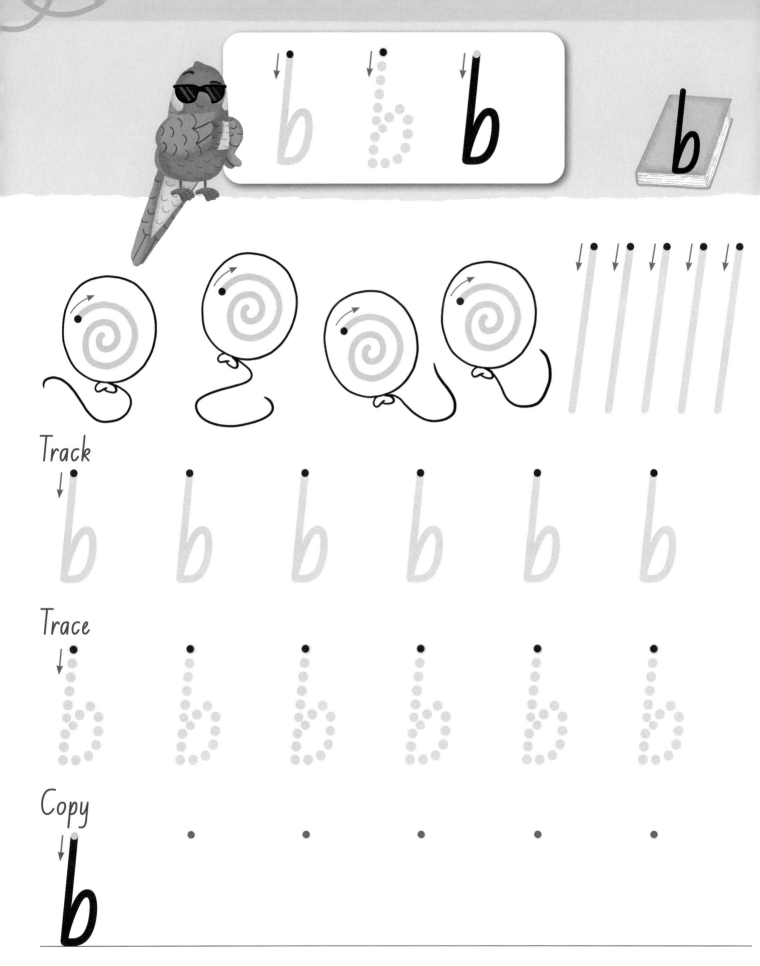

Track

Trace

Copy

OXFORD UNIVERSITY PRESS

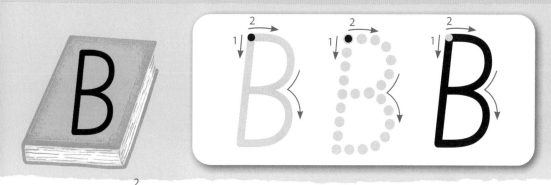

above

on

below

above

on

below

above

on

below

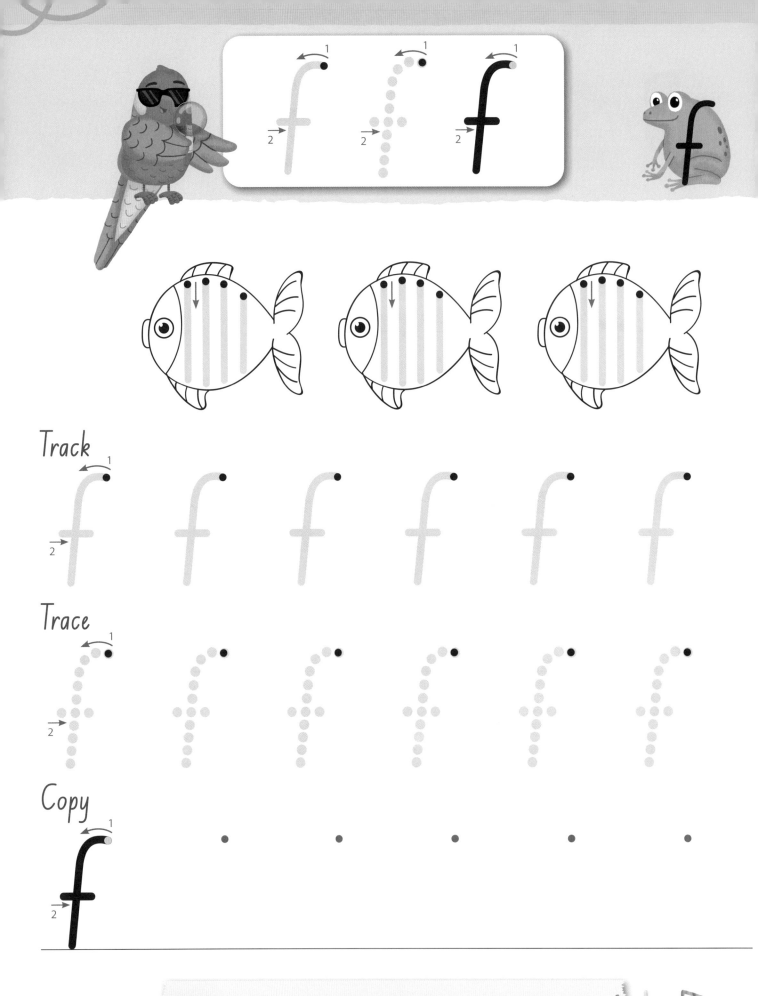

Track

Trace

Copy

Self-assessment! Ask students to circle their best lower-case f and upper-case F.
Ask them to explain the reason for their choices to you or a classmate.

above

on

below

Fast finishers Trace the word "off", and then draw something that can switch on and off.

fF 43

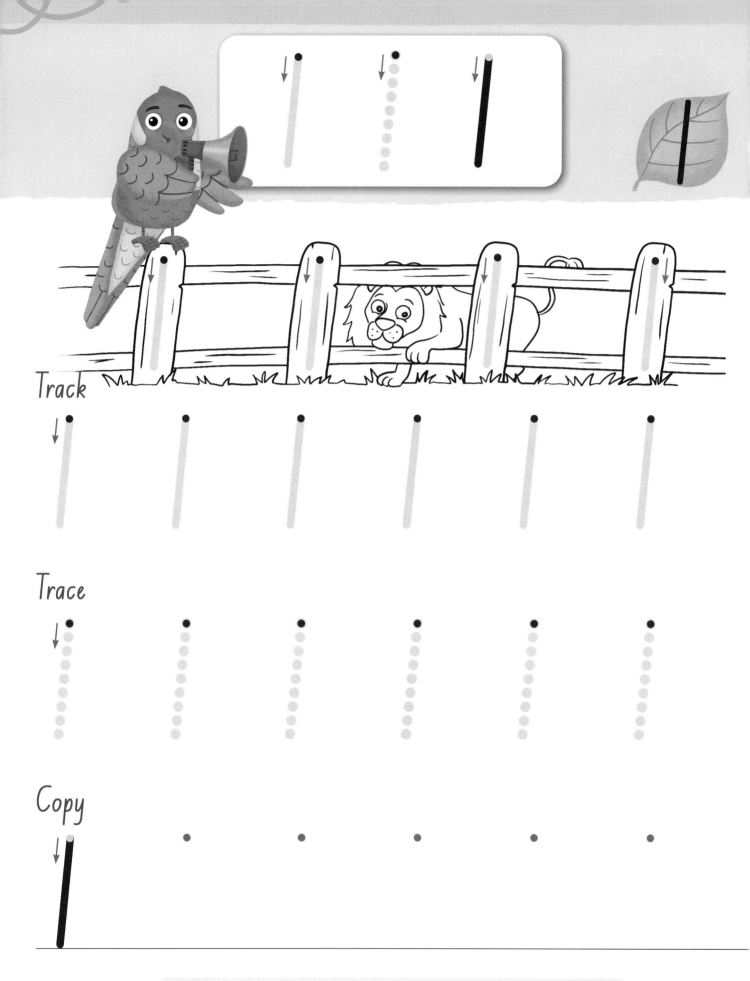

Track

Trace

Copy

OXFORD UNIVERSITY PRESS

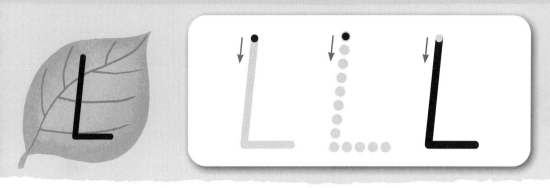

above

on

below

above

on

below

above

on

below

Fast finishers   Circle all the lower-case l's and upper-case L's in the lizard. Then colour in the lizard.

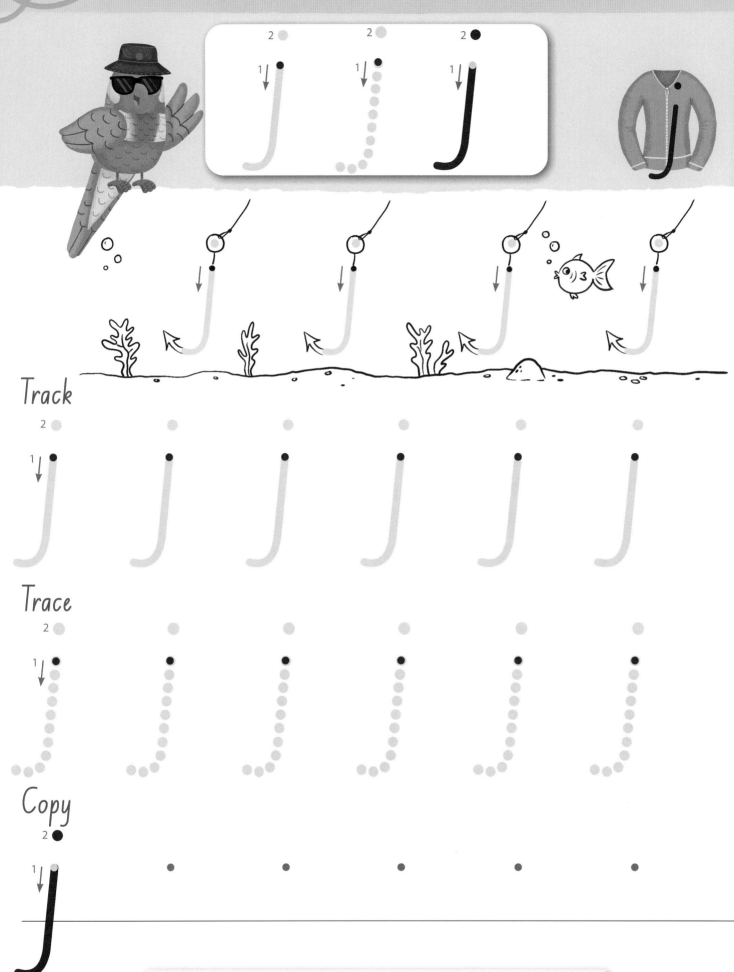

Track

Trace

Copy

Self-assessment!

Ask students to circle their best lower-case j and upper-case J.
Ask them to explain the reason for their choices to you or a classmate.

OXFORD UNIVERSITY PRESS

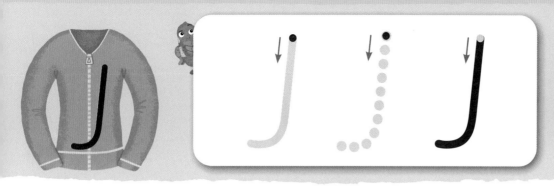

above

on

below

above

on

below

above

on

below

Fast finishers   Colour in the jugglers that have a lower-case j on them in one colour. Then colour in the remaining jugglers in different colours.

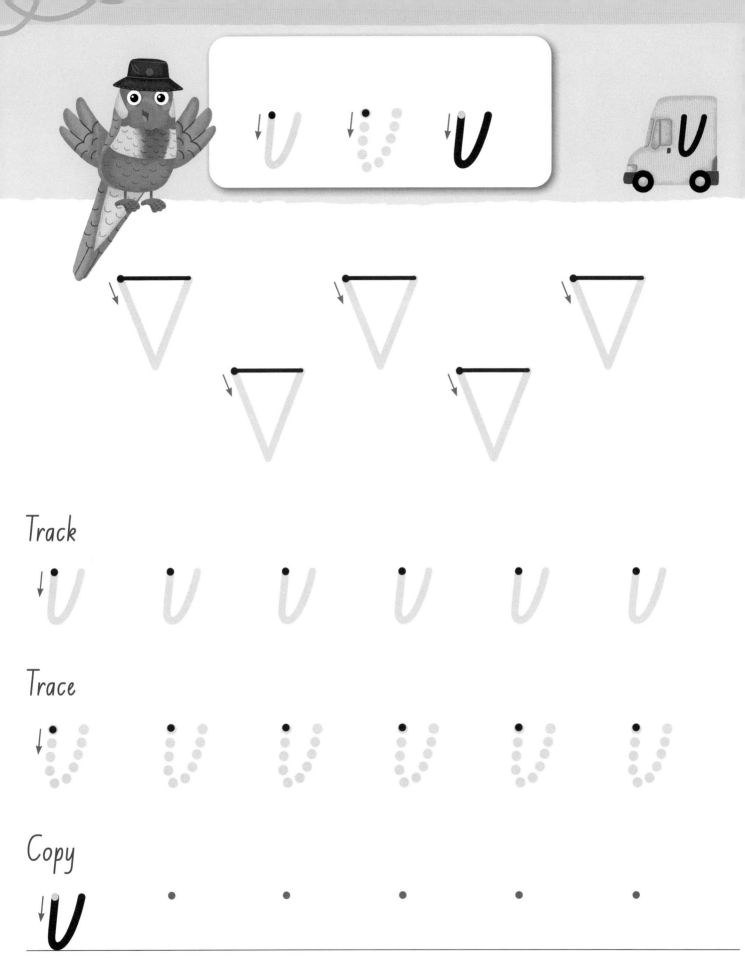

Track

Trace

Copy

OXFORD UNIVERSITY PRESS

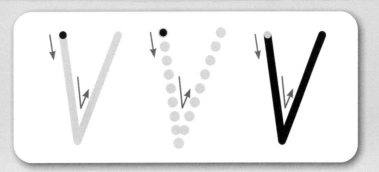

above ♪♩♪♫

on

below

above ♪♩♪♫

on

below

above ♪♩♪♫

on

below

Fast finishers   Draw a picture of your favourite vegetable.

w

Track

Trace

Copy

OXFORD UNIVERSITY PRESS

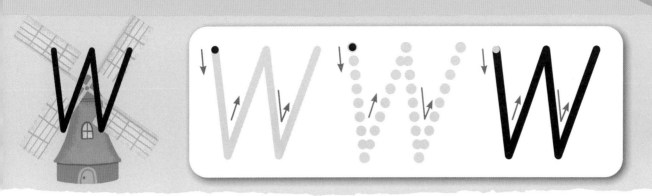

above ♪ ♩ ♫

on

below

W

above ♪ ♩ ♫

on

below

wW

above ♪ ♩ ♫

on

below

w

Fast finishers Colour in the watermelons that have a lower-case w inside them in red and green. Then colour in the remaining watermelons in different colours.

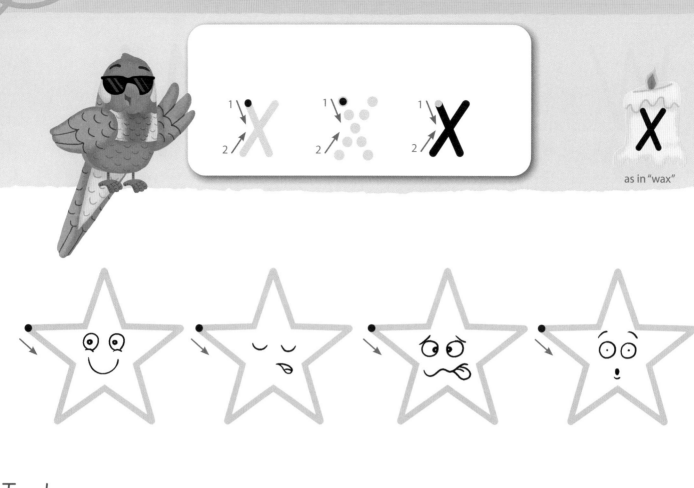

as in "wax"

Track

Trace

Copy

OXFORD UNIVERSITY PRESS

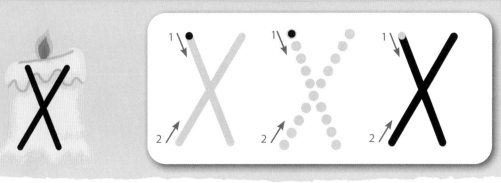

above ♪♩♫

on

below

above ♪♩♫

on

below

above ♪♩♫

on

below

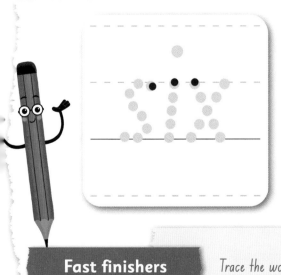

Fast finishers   *Trace the word "six", and then draw six things. For example, six faces, six bugs or six cups.*

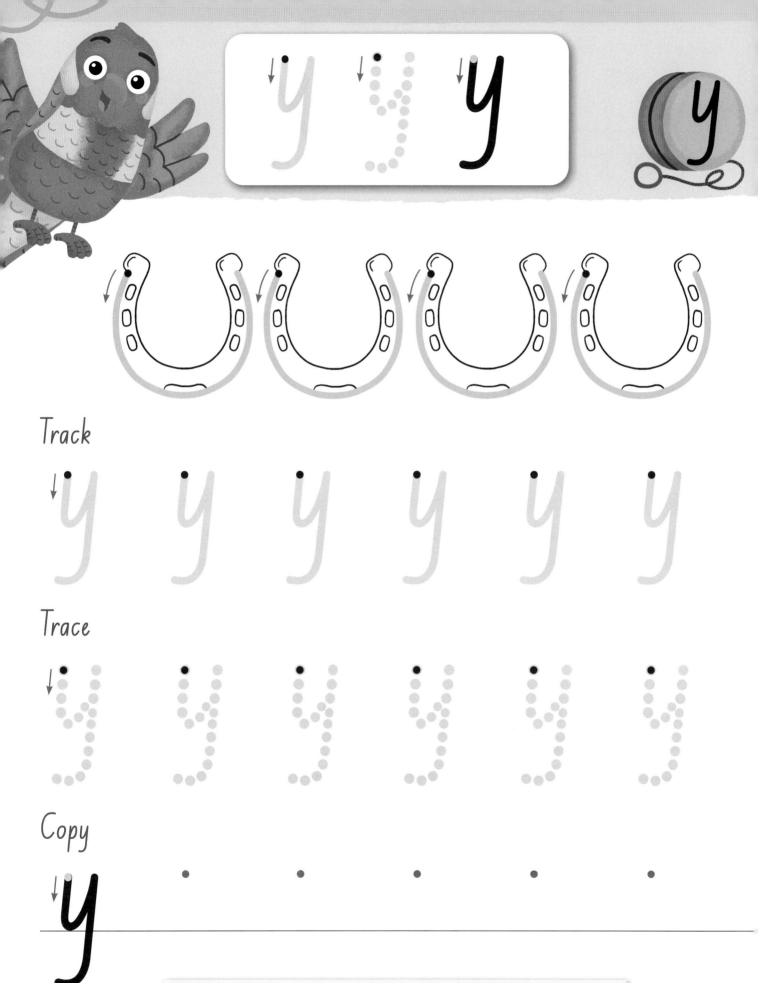

Track

Trace

Copy

Self-assessment!

Ask students to circle their best lower-case y and upper-case Y.
Ask them to explain the reason for their choices to you or a classmate.

OXFORD UNIVERSITY PRESS

above ♪♩♫

on

below

above ♪♩♫

on

below

above ♪♩♫

on

below

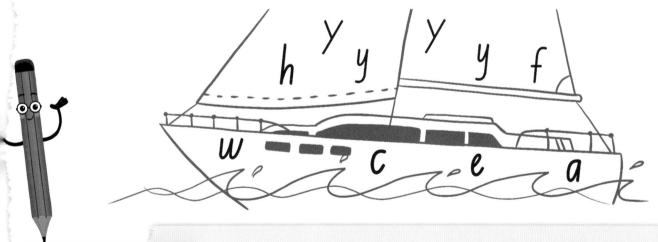

Fast finishers

Circle all the lower-case y's and upper-case Y's. What could you add to this picture? For example, a bird, the Sun or a fish.

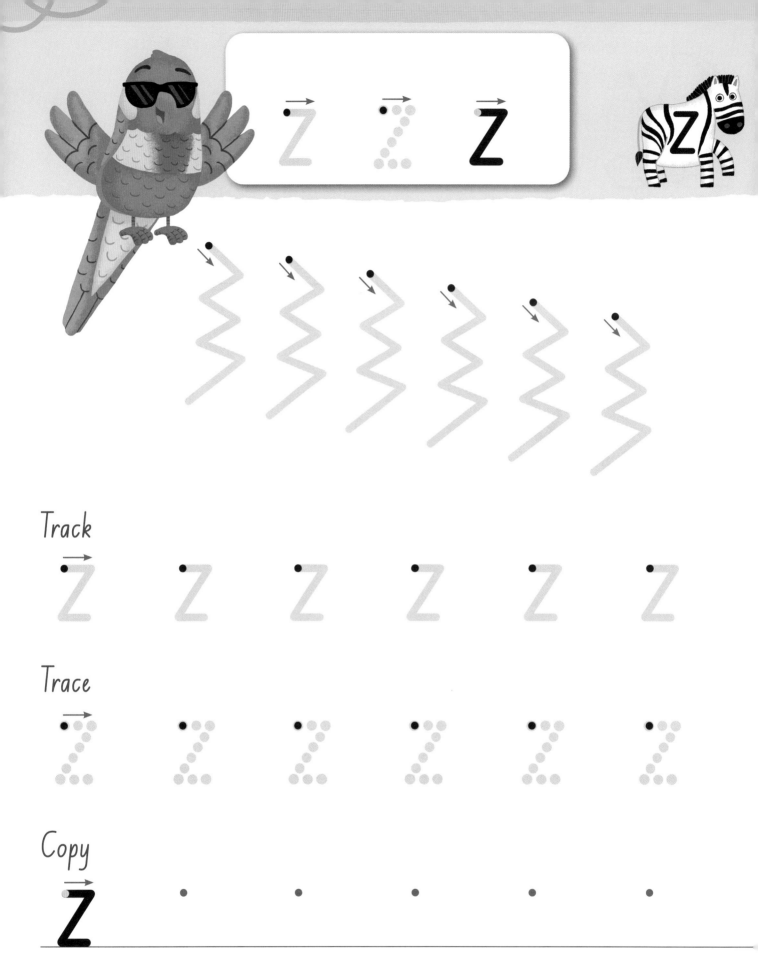

Track

Trace

Copy

Ask students to circle their best lower-case z and upper-case Z.
Ask them to explain the reason for their choices to you or a classmate.

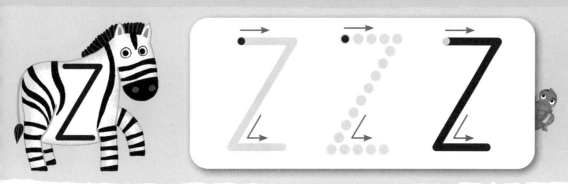

above ♪♩♫

on

below

above ♪♩♫

on

below

above ♪♩♫

on

below

Fast finishers

Trace the word "zap", and then colour in the picture of the word "zap!"

Track

Trace

Copy

q

Self-assessment!

Ask students to circle their best lower-case q and upper-case Q.
Ask them to explain the reason for their choices to you or a classmate.

OXFORD UNIVERSITY PRESS

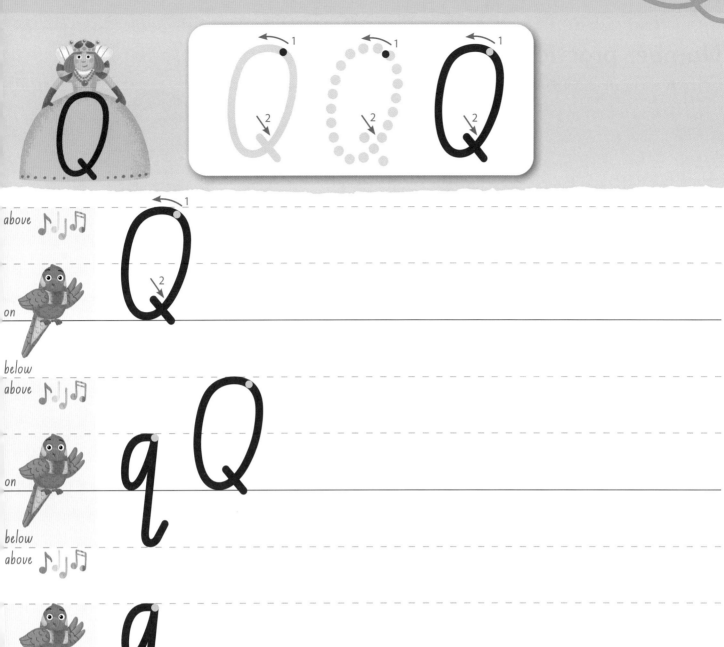

above ♪ ♩ ♫

on

below

above ♪ ♩ ♫

on

below

above ♪ ♩ ♫

on

below

Fast finishers   Trace the word "quack", and then draw a duck.

Number practice

1 1 1

1 1 1 1

2 2 2

2 2 2 2

3 3 3

3 3 3 3

OXFORD UNIVERSITY PRESS

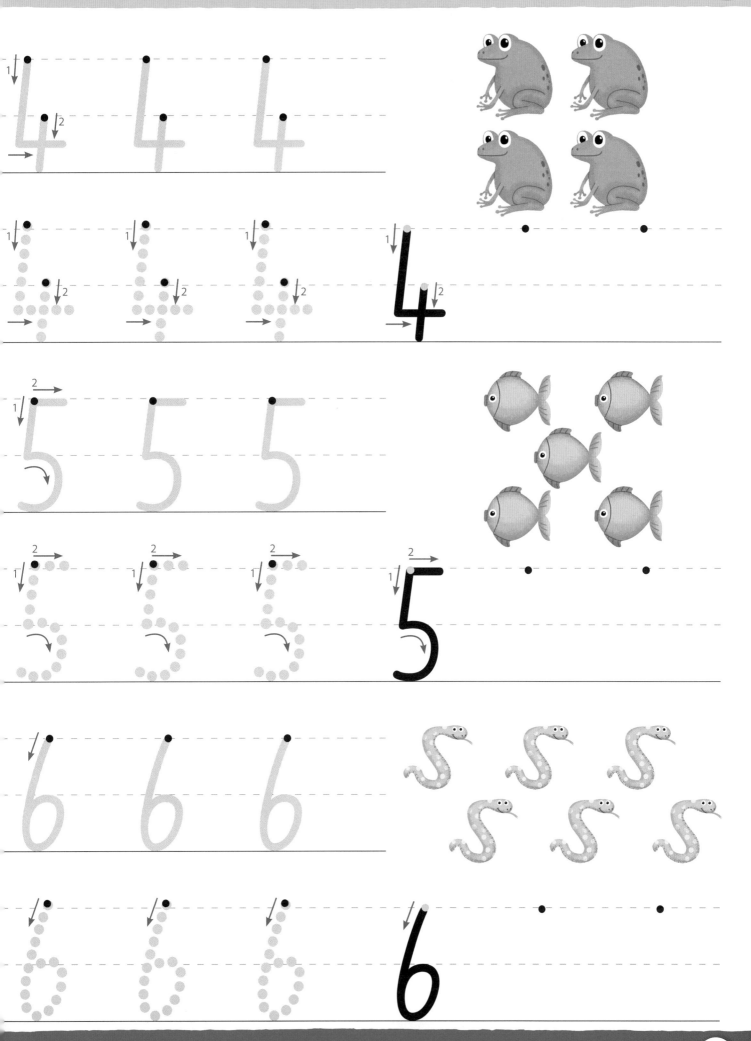

7 7 7

7 7 7

7

8 8 8

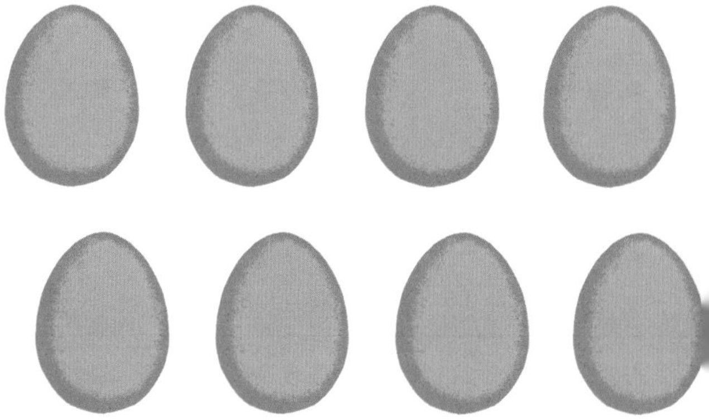

8 8 8

8

9 9 9

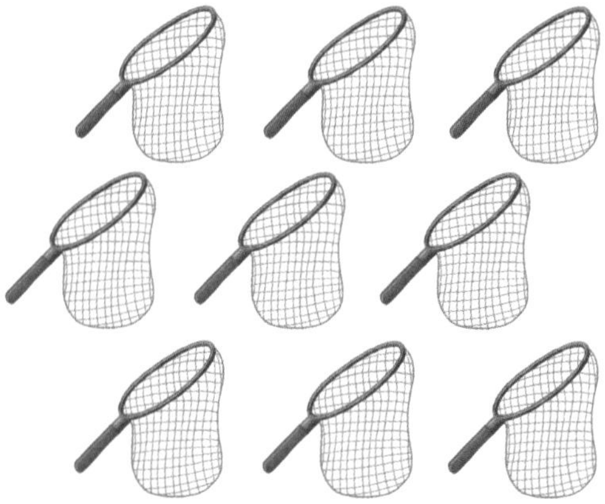

9 9 9

9

OXFORD UNIVERSITY PRESS

10 10 10

10 10 10

10

Fast finishers Choose your favourite number, and then draw a picture with that number of animals.

Number practice

Alphabet

a b c d e f g h i

j k l m n o p q r

s t u v w x y z

A B C D E F G H I

J K L M N O P Q R

S T U V W X Y Z

OXFORD UNIVERSITY PRESS